PERSUADE WITH A DIGITAL CONTENT STORY!

How Smart Business Leaders Gain a Marketing Competitive Edge

LISA APOLINSKI AND HENRY J. DEVRIES

INDIE BOOKS
INTERNATIONAL®

In loving memory of Regina Apolinski

[CONTENTS]

[LESSON 1]

YOUR DIGITAL CONTENT SUCKS— HERE'S WHY

R eady for some tough news? Your digital content sucks, and you have some statistics stacked against you. Data indicates more than 70 million blog posts are produced each month on WordPress.[1] Since WordPress powers only 35 percent of the internet,[2] a ton of digital content is being created every single day.

If that is not totally disheartening, consider the fifteen-second rule[3]: visitors to your online content will stay, on average, only fifteen seconds. Think about your digital behavior today. How quickly did you close out of a blog or link? People abandon swiftly and often because the digital content is not persuasive and there is plenty more available. With so much digital information being added every day, getting content to rise to the digital top is the Holy Grail.

There has never been a better time for sharing your digital story, and humans are hardwired for stories.

Despite all of the tough news, consumers are hungry for good digital content. Digital trend reports show while our digital consumption has dropped by three minutes a day as compared to last year, people spend nearly 40 percent of their day online.[4] That translates to spending more than one hundred days a year engaging with digital content.

There has never been a better time for sharing your digital story, and humans are hardwired for stories. Storytelling can persuade potential clients to connect with your brand on a human level, trust your brand promise, and become a repeat customer, even during uncertain economic times. That means happier clients and consistent revenue streams for organizations.

Nothing is as persuasive as storytelling with a purpose. This little book holds the keys to proven techniques for telling the great client success stories employed by Hollywood, Madison Avenue, and Wall Street.

In addition to humorous ways to remember the eight great metastories, this book reveals how to include must-have characters into each client success story, including the hero, nemesis, and mentor (spoiler: smart executives should avoid the rookie mistake of making themselves the heroes of their own client success stories).

THE SCIENCE AND ART OF STORYTELLING

In August 2008, *Scientific American Mind* published an article by Jeremy Hsu titled, "The Secrets of Storytelling: Why We Love A Good Yarn." The entire article is worth the read, but here is a concise summary.

According to Hsu, storytelling, or narrative, is a human universal. Familiar themes appear in tales throughout history and are global norms. The greatest stories—those retold through the generations and translated into other languages—do more than simply present a believable picture. These tales captivate their audiences, whose emotions can be inextricably tied to those of the characters in the stories. They connect to audiences on a human level.

By studying the narrative's power to influence beliefs, researchers are discovering how we analyze information and accept new ideas. A 2007 study by marketing researcher Jennifer Edson Escalas of Vanderbilt University found that a test audience responded more positively to advertisements in narrative form compared with straightforward ads that encouraged viewers to think logically about arguments for a product.[5] Similarly, Melanie Green of the University of North Carolina coauthored a 2006 study showing that labeling information as "fact" increased critical analysis, whereas labeling information as "fiction" had the opposite effect.[6]

Research studies in 2017 about digital storytelling in research,[7] in 2014 about the effectiveness of digital storytelling in the classroom,[8] in 2013 about six facets of storytelling,[9] and in 2011 about storytelling in education research,[10] and in 2010 about brand-consumer storytelling psychology[11] confirm the persuasive power of digital content.

People accept ideas more readily when their minds are in story mode versus when they are in an analytical mindset. By moving an audience into story mode with the right stories in the right way, organizations can dramatically increase a potential client's conversion rate.

EVERY BUSINESS HAS A STORY

"I will never forget the day Sonja called me. That call changed the course of my digital marketing agency. I discovered the power of storytelling to cut through the digital noise."

This is the mess-to-success story of Lisa Apolinski (co-author of this book). In July 2014, she had been in business for just over two years and had moderate success with her consulting agency. She quickly discovered a good way to engage with potential new clients was to lecture at conferences. Her goal was to book four speaking engagements per year. In addition, because her agency was young, she was highly committed to demonstrating her digital expertise and knowledge.

The challenge was twofold: she was breaking into a landscape that already had thousands of self-identified speakers, and she needed to create digital content that legitimized her position as a digital growth expert. She knew creating strong digital content would provide her with the expert position she sought, allow her to reach more potential clients on a regular basis, and increase her chances of being selected for speaking engagements within a competitive field.

She wanted her agency's journey to begin with a solid digital brand and strong website. With the creation of those, she took herself through the proprietary digital discovery exercise she had developed for clients. She was struggling with the question, "What do you want to be known for?" when her best friend Sonja called.

"Sonja asked me how the branding exercise was going. I was stuck on that question. What did I want to be known for? She positioned the question differently and asked when clients talk about their experiences with my agency, how did I want that conversation to go? My immediate thought was I want companies to be smarter users of digital engagement. Being my best friend, she pushed back hard and asked what would being 'smarter users' do for businesses? What exactly was in it for them?"

And that question prompted a moment of clarity on the power of storytelling. She then relayed this tale to her best friend:

When Lisa was working for a Fortune 500 company, she engaged with a digital marketing agency for a project. The agency charged a hefty sum, yet unbeknownst to her, she was doing most of the heavy lifting for the project. When she started running her own agency, she became aware of what had transpired.

In today's world, digital knowledge can be a matter of life and death for a business

---

"I felt completely taken advantage of, and I never want my clients to feel that way. I realized then what my agency stood for: empowering businesses with digital knowledge. There are many speakers and agencies that share why digital strategy is important. With my agency, I wanted clients to learn how to create digital strategies that work, which is the other critical piece of the digital puzzle."

Sonja, a scientist, wanted to know Lisa's measurement for success. Lisa knew her story would resonate regardless of where the business was located. Since she wanted to reach clients on a global scale, her goal would be to speak at one international conference by the end of 2014. Her best friend commented it was an audacious goal and would not be easy.

Sonja was right—the goal was not easy to achieve, and there were several fits and starts along the way. But Lisa was confident because she had a story to tell (several, in fact). She knew this was not a silver-bullet strategy. She needed to share the *how* behind the digital strategies and how they would work for her audience.

"I realized that because I was once in the same spot as they are today, I am them. I relate to what they are going through because I have gone through it myself. When I write articles, speak on podcasts, or lecture at conferences and universities, I always tie back to a real case to show that strategy in action—how that client got results. In a fast-paced environment, ethereal discussions do not do the audience any service. In today's world, digital knowledge can be a matter of life and death for a business."

She focused on her digital storytelling. Within two months, Lisa had her first global speaking engagement. In the five years since, Lisa has been invited to speak about digital content strategies on four continents. She has spoken to hundreds of thousands of executives on getting the most bang from their digital buck. And while peering into her crystal ball, she uses the power of storytelling to share the knowledge of what's ahead for the digital future.

The moral of the story: Clients are hardwired for stories, and this differentiator can be crucial to growing a business in the digital age.

[LESSON 2]

THE SIX-STEP DIGITAL CONTENT STORY FORMULA

Not all hope is lost. There is an easy-to-follow formula for telling a compelling digital content story.

The first person to analyze the myths, legends, tales, and stories of the world was Joseph Campbell. After his analysis, he presented a theory of what overarching storytelling formula resonates among all human societies in his now-classic 1949 book, *The Hero with a Thousand Faces*. In the early 1970s, a young filmmaker named George Lucas was writing a screenplay about space cowboys fighting against an evil empire. He happened to pick up Campbell's books and writings on the hero's journey during the course of his own research on stories and was thunderstruck to realize the film he was writing, at the time titled The Star Wars, followed the same motifs and structure.

Years later, Lucas and Campbell finally met and became good friends when PBS filmed a multipart series about Campbell's life and work at the famous Skywalker Ranch.

There's a formula for that. The best way to continue success is to use a formula that provides a magical addition: *repeatability*. Why recreate the wheel over and over if you can use a formula so your repeated efforts become effortless? Here is your new weapon in your digital content arsenal: the *Six-Step Digital Content Story Formula*. Each step is critical for persuasive storytelling—so let's dive deeper into those steps.

SIX-STEP DIGITAL CONTENT STORY FORMULA

1 START AND DESCRIBE **MAIN** CHARACTER

2 INTRODUCE **NEMESIS** CHARACTER

3 CUE **MENTOR** CHARACTER

4 KEEP STORIES **CHARACTER-CENTERED**

5 HAVE MAIN CHARACTER **SUCCEED**

6 SHARE **MORAL** OF THE STORY

Start with a main character. Every client success story starts with someone who wants something. For your story, this is the executive at your client organization—either a real one or an ideal one. Be sure your main character is likable—describe some of their good qualities, some of their struggles, and make them relatable—so the reader or listener will root for them.

Introduce a nemesis character. Stories need conflict to be interesting. The nemesis does not necessarily have to be human. Define the person, institution, or condition that stands in the character's path to business success.

REDUCED BUDGET IS A TYPICAL ORGANIZATIONAL NEMESIS

For many organizations needing to hit net revenue goals (or simply to reduce expenses), a budget cut becomes the first go-to strategy. However, sales or revenue goals are hardly ever adjusted.

This scenario is a common occurrence for organizations, with many department heads having to try to hit goals with fewer resources. This classic nemesis character certainly gets in the way of achieving the sales or revenue goal. With a budget cut lurking around every corner and at every quarterly review, most department heads will encounter this bad guy at some point in their careers.

Enter the mentor character. Heroes always need help on their journey. They need to work with a wise person. So, cue the guru. This is where you come in. Be the voice of wisdom and experience in your client success story, since that is what your client engages you to do.

Keep the story character-centric. When discussing the benefits of working with you (the mentor), be sure to keep that discussion focused on what the hero (client) gained from the interaction. If the story focuses on what the mentor did, the center moves from character to plot (and off the success of the hero).

Show that the hero clearly succeeds. Setting up the finish line and then showing the hero (client) cross the finish line is a key step that sometimes gets missed. In seven of the eight great metastories, the main character needs to succeed, with one exception: tragedy. The tragic story is told as a cautionary tale. (Great for teaching lessons or lectures, but not great for persuading future clients.)

Give the prospects the moral of the story. Don't count on the listeners to get the message. The digital storyteller's final job is to come right out and tell them what the story means.

When you start to create your digital content stories, know what specific kind of client success story you are telling. Human brains seem to be programmed to relate to one of eight great metastories: monster, underdog, comedy, tragedy, mystery, quest, rebirth, and escape.

Start now and begin building a collection of client success stories that you have played a role in. You do not lead with the story; you close with the client success story to improve your lead conversion rate and to help the prospect envision themselves as a successful client.

MAGIC WORDS AND PHRASES

Think of the moral of your story as one of your magic words and phrases. It drives home the story purpose and serves to help market your brand and what it stands for. If someone said, "People first; then money; then things," you know they are sharing the magic phrase from American financier Suze Orman. Magic words and phrases also signal the end of the story; for example, "And they lived happily ever after."

EXAMPLE: JOHN'S MONSTER STORY

[This is a mess-to-success client story from coauthor Lisa Apolinski.]

> *John is the owner of a small manufacturing company—a company he has built over the last twenty-five years. The concept of online reputation management had been the last thing on his mind until he found out how quickly his company's reputation could be affected by a past business relationship.*

> *"Being a smaller company that has flown under the digital radar and had no bad PR, I hadn't even considered digital association," he said. "But that naïve thinking almost led to our company's downfall."*

> *John, at sixty-two, had only dipped his toe in the digital waters. He had a website and a couple of social channels where new products and specials were shared. For his company, he considered digital*

engagement as an afterthought. After all, his clients had worked with him for years and knew his products were of great quality, and the company used more traditional methods to take orders. But then one of his larger clients had a major PR disaster. What made the situation worse was there was a tangential association of this PR/social issue with vendors in the manufacturing industry, including his company.

"Within forty-eight hours of the PR issue with this client, we discovered that there were hundreds of mentions of our organization attached to that digital conversation," John explained. "We had not been monitoring what was being said about us. And then suddenly, there was a tsunami of posts on our website and social media channels saying that since we had provided products to this client, we were guilty by association. The digital firestorm was so fast, and we were woefully unprepared for the fallout."

When John came to Lisa and her digital consulting agency, he had tried to handle the situation himself but had missed opportunities to address the issue and provide digital means to take further questions and conversations privately. Many clients had already pulled orders based on digital perception and what they believed was a lackluster digital stand. Both a short- and long-term digital solution had to be created, and fast, to prevent further revenue erosion.

The short-term solution was the most uncomfortable for John. "I thought by sidestepping the issue, it would go away. I was shocked by how that decision actually made the digital scrutiny more intense. Sharing my thoughts on the matter was the most difficult—I was putting myself in a completely vulnerable position. But this company is my heart and soul, and once I spoke from that place, the digital conversation shifted, and we saw more support," he said.

John first learned content that shares thoughts on the situation in a raw and vulnerable way opens the digital conversation. Once the initial PR calamity had passed, the company continued to take and share key actions that demonstrated its commitment to combatting the social issue that had initially been tied to the company. In addition, a clear and documented process for monitoring and addressing the company's online reputation was created.

"I hate to admit it, but we had our heads in the sand when it came to our digital reputation," he said. "My entire organization now recognizes how important our digital health is. We are still working on getting our reputation back to prior levels, and are more diligent in keeping the online reputation we have worked so hard to create intact. Many of our clients came back, and we attracted new ones, allowing digital lemons to be turned into lemonade. Initially, this lesson left a sour taste but

ended up being crucial in how we used our digital engagement."

The moral of the story: A digital PR disaster can happen to any company at any time, so have a plan. "Your company doesn't even have to be the one to make the PR error, but it could be the one paying for it."

This story may be scarier than *Star Wars*. John's story is to the point and follows the formula.

Start with a main character. The main character is manufacturing company owner John. We like John because he has worked to build his company and has suffered an undeserved misfortune—tangential association with a client who stepped in digital PR doodoo.

Have a nemesis character. In this case, the nemesis is the digital community out for blood.

Bring in a mentor character. Since this was her client, Lisa was the mentor character.

Be a character-centric storyteller. This story, where John had to fight to keep his company from being wrongfully destroyed by a bad digital PR story, moved to a few actions he took and his "lessons learned."

Have the hero succeed. John says, "I got uncomfortable in order to make the digital engagement stronger. By sharing my human story as a digital story, my company became human and relatable. While this was something that was different from our prior digital engagement, we actually experienced an increase in our client base." We can see a bustling manufacturing floor with new orders coming in. In storytelling, we call an image like that *crossing a visible finish line.*

Give the audience the moral of the story. John says, "Do not let the fear of the unknown stand in your way." With a digital PR plan, the monster doesn't have to destroy the company you have built.

FOUR WAYS TO BECOME BETTER AT DIGITAL STORIES

To increase digital engagement, move beyond facts to tell when you can use stories to sell. Experts and thought leaders are typically great storytellers.

"Trying to influence people by using words to appeal to their intellect isn't enough," says Dr. Paul Homoly. "We need stories."

As an acclaimed educator for over thirty years, Homoly is known for his innovative and practical approach to dentistry. He retired from clinical practice in 1995 and now devotes his full-time focus to training, coaching, consulting, and authoring.

Here is some advice from Homoly on storytelling:

Keep Stories Short. "A good way to think about stories is to picture an artist at a street fair who's perched on a stool, wearing a beret," says Homoly. "He has an easel, drawing pencils, or a handful of dry erase markers, and for twenty bucks, he'll draw your caricature. A few lines here, a few curves there, and the artist captures the *gist* of the features that make you distinct. Your mind fills in the rest of the details. Great stories are oral caricatures. A few visual and emotional words paint just enough of the picture for your mind to fill in the missing elements."

Keep Stories In The Present Tense, If Appropriate. "You've probably noticed that many great stories are told in the present tense," says Homoly. "That is done on purpose because it helps you experience the story as if it's happening right now. Switching to the present tense draws the listener into the story because your verbs are active, and your language is more alive. I'm reliving it in the moment as I tell it, as opposed to narrating the past. Reliving the events in your story makes it easier for you to feel it, which makes it easy for your listeners to feel it too."

Keep Stories Visual. "When done well, the language of your story creates images in your audience's mind," says Homoly. "You'll discover that well-told stories are an auditory *and visual experience* for the listener. Listeners are actually picturing your points, which means they're fully engaged, which means they're giving you their full attention."

Keep Stories Emotional To You. "It's important to select stories that are emotional to you, so you feel them while you tell them," says Homoly. "You are trying to move people to action—to make a decision, follow your advice, take their medicine. To move people into action, you need to move them emotionally."

THREE MUST-HAVE CHARACTERS

Every client success story needs a hero (think main character), a nemesis, and a mentor. If you are familiar with *The Karate Kid*, the main character is Danny LaRusso, the nemesis is karate and classmate rival Johnny Lawrence, and the mentor is the quiet yet wise Mr. Miyagi.

If the first three *Star Wars* movies are more your brand of vodka, then we are talking about Luke Skywalker as the hero, Darth Vader as the nemesis, and Jedi Knight Obi-Wan Kenobi and later Jedi Master Yoda as the mentors. (My favorite mentor advice from Yoda is: "Do or do not. There is no *try*." That line was even used in an episode of *The Big Bang Theory*.)

Here are more details on utilizing the first three steps of the storytelling formula:

Start With A Hero. This is the main character. Dorothy, Sherlock Holmes, and Buffy the Vampire Slayer have something in common. They are each the protagonist who propels the story. The first sentence of your story begins with the name of the main character and a clear picture of what he or she wants.

Next, Introduce The Nemesis. What is preventing the main character from getting what he or she wants? Stories are not engaging if they don't have conflict, so the main character needs opposition from another character. Professor Moriarty is a master nemesis. So are vampire Spike and the Wicked Witch of the West in Oz ("I'll get you, my pretty, and your little dog, too!"). Often, the word "antagonist" is a better term. In business storytelling, common nemeses are often inappropriate business decisions, the competition, or a bad economy.

Then Add The Mentor. This is where you come in. Heroes can't do it on their own. If they could, they would have done so already. They need outside expertise or training. Sometimes, they need guidance to show them the way or get them back on the right road. The hero needs the voice of experience and wisdom. Glinda the Good Witch, Dr. Watson, and Giles the librarian and Guardian of the Slayer, are there to fill this critical need.

DON'T FALL FOR THE HERO ROLE

In our work, clients often object to being cast as the mentor instead of the hero. "What we did should be defined as heroic—we saved that client," they say.

"So," we ask them, "if you cast yourself as the hero, what role does your client automatically take on as the opposite?"

The answer is "the damsel in distress." (By the way, in *The Karate Kid*, the damsel is Ali Mills. She is also the prize for the winner in the conflict.)

Your clients do not want to cast themselves into a story as the damsel in distress, nor be the prize at the end of the story. However, if the role of hero is taken, that is how they will show up and respond to your communication.

Clients want to see themselves as the hero who had the insight to recognize and listen to the right mentor who helps them overcome the nemesis.

Let us repeat this for emphasis: If you want to attract more clients, then your clients must be the heroes, or main characters, of all your digital stories (save just one). In the mentor role, your organization will have long-term relevancy for your clients. Your clients will always be in need of a mentor who helps *them* save the day (regardless of economic conditions). And with you in the mentor role, they will know who to call to guide them to victory each and every time.

If you want to attract more clients, then your clients must be the heroes, or main characters, of all your digital stories.

SO HOW DO YOU BRING THESE CHARACTERS INTO YOUR DIGITAL STORY?

Start your digital story by introducing the main character—a character similar to your prospective client. The character should have some similar qualities, like gender, length of time in his or her position, or similar type of role in the company.

Make the main character likable. Make people who hear/read the story want to root for the main character.

Next, introduce the nemesis or problem. In one of coauthor Henry DeVries's stories, he labels a bad economy as "the wolf at the door." If you can use a person to represent the issue—a technique called "personification"—great. However, in the business world, the presented problem is typically a situation (caused by a person). Whatever is keeping the hero from reaching his/her goal is your nemesis character.

Finally, cast yourself as the mentor or wise character of the story. With your training or advice, your hero/client will overcome the nemesis problem. You are the voice of wisdom and experience.

A FEW FAMOUS HEROES, VILLAINS, AND MENTORS TO GET YOUR CREATIVE JUICES FLOWING

Heroes/Main Characters

- Luke Skywalker from the original *Star Wars* trilogy
- King Arthur
- Indiana Jones from *Indiana Jones and The Raiders of the Lost Ark*
- Scarlett O'Hara from *Gone with the Wind*
- Atticus Finch from *To Kill a Mockingbird*
- John Galt from *Atlas Shrugged*

- Harry Potter from *Harry Potter and the Sorcerer's Stone*
- Eliza Doolittle from *My Fair Lady*
- Rocky Balboa from *Rocky*
- Katniss Everdeen from *The Hunger Games*
- James Bond from every single *James Bond* novel and film ever
- Cinderella from *Cinderella*
- Lisbeth Salander from *The Girl with the Dragon Tattoo*
- Sherlock Holmes from the *Sherlock Holmes* stories by Sir Arthur Conan Doyle
- Roy Hobbs from *The Natural*
- Shaun from *Shaun of the Dead*

Villains/Nemeses

- Darth Vader from the original *Star Wars* trilogy
- Wicked Witch of the West from *The Wonderful Wizard of Oz*

- Hannibal Lecter from *Silence of the Lambs*

- Norman Bates from *Psycho*

- Big Brother from *1984*

- Apollo Creed from *Rocky*

- Evil stepmother from *Cinderella*

- Professor Moriarty from the *Sherlock Holmes* stories by Sir Arthur Conan Doyle

- Judge Banner from *The Natural*

- Zombies from *Shaun of the Dead*

Mentors
- Glinda the Good Witch from *The Wonderful Wizard of Oz*

- Jim from *Huckleberry Finn*

- Yoda from *Star Wars*

- Professor Henry Higgins from *My Fair Lady*

- Mickey from *Rocky*

- Fairy Godmother from *Cinderella*

- Dr. John Watson from the *Sherlock Holmes* stories by Sir Arthur Conan Doyle
- Friar Tuck from *Robin Hood*
- Iris from *The Natural*
- Shaun's stepdad, Phillip, from *Shaun of the Dead* (thought he was the nemesis, huh?)
- Iago from *Othello* (because not all mentors are good mentors)

TRYING TO HAVE YOUR HERO CAKE AND EAT IT TOO

When creating a digital content story, many organizations make the mistake of casting themselves in the role of hero. That casting automatically creates the audience's role of "damsel in distress." But there is another potential landmine waiting, especially if that message is received poorly.

During the coronavirus pandemic, Trader Joe's and McDonald's stepped up to provide paid sick leave to their hourly employees. Whole Foods shared a different message during the crisis. The company asked for employees to use a sick leave policy developed when Whole Foods was first starting. This policy allowed employees to share PTO with others, so time off would not go unused.

Before this digital story hit, the nemesis in the digital world was the coronavirus. That nemesis had no form, could be anywhere and was something people felt powerless to fight. With this leaked employee memo, there was suddenly a new nemesis to cast: Amazon (and Whole Foods owner) CEO, Jeff Bezos. And this is a popular nemesis: a rich, out of touch, older, white male.

The digital backlash to this policy was fast and plentiful. People now had a real target on which to focus their anger, frustration, and fear. This was probably not the intended result of the message from Whole Foods. In the letter from Whole Foods CEO John Mackey, he tried to cast himself as the hero—the one who would swoop in and save the day with a paid sick leave policy.

The main issue was this message was not one a hero would say. Batman does not drive into town and then tell the people of Gotham City to pull together to beat Joker. Batman takes Joker head-on. This letter asked the employees to take on the problem of paid sick leave—something the company should be addressing on behalf of the employees.

Companies cannot have their hero cake and eat it too. The best digital content story avoids this trap by taking on the role of mentor.

EIGHT GREAT STORIES

The first step is always a conversation. A company needs to listen carefully and respond appropriately. Never start with the story; begin by listening to the client first.

Leaving space for someone to share is vital during client interaction. The first reaction to silence is to fill up space. This is where the opportunity lies for your client to share the essence of the issue. Allow the silence, even if the client has initially said no. In many instances, a negative response to support or assistance is a developed reaction. By providing time for the client to register the interaction, more information may be shared.

Facts and data appeal to one part of the mind, but stories provide a shortcut to the emotional part of the mind. That is where decisions are made.

Remember this tip: open-ended questions create conversations. Yes/no questions kill them.

After you have listened, ask the client if you can tell them a story about someone who was in a similar situation. Facts and data appeal to one part of the mind, but stories provide a shortcut to the emotional part of the mind. That is where decisions are made.

WHICH OF THE EIGHT GREAT STORIES SHOULD YOU USE?

You have listened and now are ready to tell your story. But which story should you use? As outlined earlier, there are eight great metastories that humans tell (and want to hear) repeatedly. What type of story are you telling? Almost all movies and literature follow these eight basic story structures.

This chapter is based on *The Seven Basic Plots: Why We Tell Stories*, a 2004 book by British journalist Christopher Booker, which took him more than thirty years to research and write. The work is a Jungian-influenced analysis of stories and their psychological meaning. We compared Booker's eight categories and discovered the same rules apply to the greatest business nonfiction books of all time, too.

Here are Booker's eight categories:

Monster. A terrifying, all-powerful, life-threatening monster who the hero must confront in a fight to the death. An example of this plot is seen in *Beowulf*, *Jaws*, *Jack and the Beanstalk*, and *Dracula*. Most business books follow this plot. There is some monster problem in the workplace, and this is how you attack it.

Business book examples:

- *The One-Minute Manager* by Ken Blanchard and Spencer Johnson
- *Slay the E-Mail Monster* by Mike Valentine and Lynn Coffman
- *The E-Myth Revisited* by Michael Gerber
- *Whale Hunting* by Tom Searcy and Barbara Weaver Smith
- *The Five Dysfunctions of a Team* by Patrick Lencioni
- *Growing Your Business* by Mark LeBlanc

Underdog. Someone who seemed to the world to be quite commonplace is shown to have been hiding a second, more exceptional self within. Think *The Ugly Duckling*, *Cinderella*, *David and Goliath*, *Jane Eyre*, and *Superman*. The business books in this category discuss how people raised themselves up from nothing to success—your typical rags-to-riches stories.

Business book examples:

- *Moneyball* by Michael Lewis
- *The Art of the Start* by Guy Kawasaki
- *Up the Organization* by Robert Townsend
- *Grinding it Out* by Ray Kroc

Comedy. Comedy and tragedy aren't about being funny or sad; any story can be funny or sad. Comedy and tragedy are about problem-solving.

If the main character tries to solve a problem with a wacky idea, that is a comedy. Think of the movies: *Wedding Crashers*, *We're the Millers*, *Tootsie*, and *Some Like It Hot*. Following general chaos of misunderstanding, the characters tie themselves and each other into a knot that seems almost unbearable; however, to universal relief, everyone and everything gets sorted out, bringing about the happy ending. Shakespeare's comedies also come to mind, such as *Comedy of Errors* and *All's Well that Ends Well,* as do Jane Austen's novels, like *Emma* and *Sense and Sensibility*.

Business book examples:

- *2030: What Really Happens to America* by Albert Brooks

- *A Whack on the Side of the Head* by Roger von Oech

- *Purple Cow* by Seth Godin

- *How I Lost My Virginity* by Sir Richard Branson

- *Swim with the Sharks Without Getting Eaten Alive* by Harvey Mackay

Tragedy. This story is about solving a problem by going against the laws of nature, society, or God. Through some flaw or lack of self-understanding, a character is increasingly drawn into a fatal course of action which inexorably leads to disaster. *King Lear*, *Othello*, *The Godfather*, *The Great Gatsby*, *Madame Bovary*, *The Picture of Dorian Gray*, *Breaking Bad*, *Scarface*, and *Bonnie and Clyde*—these are all flagrantly tragic.

Business book examples:

- *Too Big to Fail* by Aaron Sorkin
- *Barbarians at the Gate* by Brian Burrough and John Helyar
- *Liar's Poker* by Michael Lewis

Quest. From the moment the hero learns of the priceless goal, he sets out on a hazardous journey to reach it. Examples are seen in *The Odyssey*, *Star Wars*, *The Count of Monte Cristo*, *The Sting*, *The Italian Job*, and *Raiders of the Lost Ark*.

Business book examples:

- *The HP Way* by David Packard
- *In Search of Excellence* by Tom Peters
- *Influence* by Robert Cialdini
- *How to Win Friends and Influence People* by Dale Carnegie
- *How to Close a Deal Like Warren Buffett* by Tom Searcy and Henry DeVries
- *The Big Short* by Michael Lewis

- *Weathering the Digital Storm* by Lisa Apolinski

Escape. The hero or heroine (main character) and a few companions leave familiar surroundings for another world completely cut off from the first. While it is at first wonderful, there is a sense of increasing peril. After a dramatic escape, they return to the familiar world where they began.

Alice in Wonderland and *The Lord of the Rings* are obvious examples, but *The Wonderful Wizard of Oz* and *Gone with the Wind* also embody this basic plotline.

Business book examples:

- *The Prodigal Executive* by Bruce Heller
- *The Innovator's Dilemma* by Clayton Christensen
- *How I Raised Myself from Failure to Success in Selling* by Frank Bettger

Rebirth. There is a mounting sense of doom as a dark force approaches the hero until it emerges completely, holding the hero in its deadly grip.

Only after a time, when it seems that the dark force has triumphed, does the reversal take place. The hero is redeemed, usually through the life-giving power of love. Many fairy tales take this shape. Think *American Hustle*, *Harry Potter*, *A Christmas Carol*, and *It's a Wonderful Life*.

Business book examples:

- *Out of Crisis* by W. Edwards Deming
- *Reengineering the Corporation* by Michael Hammer and James Champy
- *Seabiscuit* by Lauren Hillenbrand (technically a sports memoir)

Mystery. In his book, Booker adds an eighth plot, a newcomer that has appeared from the time of Edgar Allan Poe. From the Sherlock Holmes stories to the *CSI* TV series franchise, this basic plot involves solving a riddle and has gained immense popularity since the mid-1800s.

Business book examples:

- *Good to Great* by Jim Collins

- *Think and Grow Rich* by Napoleon Hill
- *The Secret* by Rhonda Byrne
- *Who Moved My Cheese?* by Spencer Johnson
- *The Monk and the Riddle* by Randy Komisar with Kent Lineback
- *Cracking the Personality Code* by Dana and Ellen Borowka

HOW TO APPLY THE EIGHT GREAT STORIES

To improve your understanding and get your creative gears turning, the following chapters give you more examples of the eight great stories.

At the end of each of the eight chapters, you will find a box with an example of how to apply the principles from that type of story to your client presentations. Feel free to adapt the example to fit your style. Or even better, develop a story of your own from your experiences.

Ideally, you will want to have one or two stories up your sleeve for each genre of story types.

This way, you are ready for most story-type scenarios that a client may find themselves in.

EVERY COMPANY HAS A POWERFUL STORY

Many organizations might not recognize this important fact: Every company has a powerful story.

Perhaps in reading this, you wonder what your story could possibly be. If you are not sure what your story is, look at your "moment."

Before an organization had a name, registration, or any digital presence, someone had to have a thought—that first moment when the idea of a new organization came into being.

What led up to that thought? Where were you? What month and year? What time of day? When you think of that moment, what visual or smell or sound comes to mind? Who were you speaking with? Were you standing or sitting?

By taking yourself back to that specific moment in time with key components and recreating the day going into that moment, you are building your own story.

First, you will be able to add visual details for your audience to place themselves into the scene.

Next, you will quickly identify your nemesis character (because something was not going right for you to decide to leap on your own into the unknown).

You will also identify your mentor character (someone said something to you to create a new possibility that did not previously exist).

Your story will be character-centric (because you are describing the moment of creation, which is based on your thoughts and feelings).

Since you now have a company, you have crossed your finish line.

And you can add in a final sentence that clearly states the moral of your story.

The story does not have to be one-of-a-kind or spectacular. It simply needs to reflect your journey—because, while your journey is unique to you, it has elements relatable to others.

The relatability and human journey provide an amazing story that can inspire others, and that story is within you. You just need to find it and share it.

[LESSON 5]

MONSTER STORIES

A horrifying monster must be killed. This is a kill-or-be-killed situation. Nothing matters more than overcoming the monster. Here is an example from coauthor Lisa Apolinski:

> We have never seen a monster problem like COVID-19.
>
> In terms of characteristics of a nemesis, COVID-19 presents as a supervillain. The virus is invisible and can be on any surface. People can be infected and not show symptoms for several days. The virus can strike anyone at any time.
>
> The impact has been more than just on health. The virus has upended everyday life, work, businesses, the global economy—

even the ability to purchase toilet paper and groceries.

Banks have been tapped to provide much-needed loan assistance through an unprecedented stimulus package for small businesses. On Friday, April 3, 2020, several banks launched digital platforms just for loan applications to keep businesses afloat.

The process was less than smooth, and one bank manager, Patricia, took note.

"The immense backlash on the process was because of not managing expectations through communication," said Patricia. "As a smaller bank, we could not afford the hit our reputation would take if we did not develop a different type of communication. But we needed someone to lead us in this charge."

Patricia called digital growth expert Lisa Apolinski.

"My bank CEO has assigned a goal to have 90 percent report a positive experience with the process, regardless of the loan application outcome. I know this is an aggressive number. How do I help our bank achieve this goal?"

"This situation, while very difficult, provides an opportunity for your financial institution to help clients to survive," said Lisa Apolinski. "Imagine, that because of your guidance, a small business owner is able to navigate a very difficult time and a process that is most likely unfamiliar to them. This will not be easy. Are you willing to take it on?"

Patricia was not completely convinced that this strategy would work, but she had a target and so was willing to put in the effort to get there.

The problem was not the process. The problem was how that process was communicated and how help was applied along the way. Processes for financial institutions are regulated, so the issue became one of sharing that process and providing steps businesses could take to move through the application process as quickly as possible. Knowledge became the weapon that this bank provided to small business owners.

Incoming applicants were segmented through a newly created landing page, and communication was developed to assist business owners, from informational emails to communication on small business best practices for managing cash flow.

Patricia gave me a call several weeks later. "This communication strategy was unlike anything we had done in the past. Through an online survey, applicants gave a 91 percent positive rating to our bank's process. I was surprised since this process was followed by all financial institutions. By focusing on guidance and education to small business communities, our clients were empowered to act."

The moral of the story: your role in your story shapes how you engage with your clients.

CLASSIC EXAMPLES

Monster problem stories are a staple of literature, plays, and films. Here are a few examples:

Jaws (novel by Peter Benchley, film by Steven Spielberg). It's a hot summer on Amity Island, a small community whose main business is beach tourism. When new Sheriff Martin Brody (main character) discovers the remains of a shark attack victim, his first inclination is to close the beach to swimmers. That would be bad for tourism, and the idea doesn't sit well with Mayor Larry Vaughn and several of the local businessmen (minor nemesis characters). Brody backs down, to his regret, as that weekend, a young boy is killed by the great white shark (nemesis). The dead boy's mother puts out a bounty on the shark, and Amity is soon swamped with amateur hunters and fishermen hoping to cash in on the reward. A local fisherman with extensive shark-hunting experience, Quint (mentor), offers to hunt down the creature for a hefty fee. Soon Quint, Brody, and Matt Hooper from the oceanographic institute are at sea, hunting the great white shark. A shark is killed, but that is not the real monster. As Brody succinctly surmises after their first encounter with the creature, they're going to need a bigger boat.

Monster problem stories are a staple of literature, plays, and films.

Beowulf (Norse tale from the Middle Ages). In a medieval land, an outpost is surrounded by an army. A flesh-eating creature called Grendel (nemesis) is killing off all who live in the outpost. That is, until the arrival of Beowulf (main character), a mysterious mercenary who offers Hrothgar, the outpost's ruler, help to hunt Grendel. Beowulf kills Grendel, but that is not the real monster (notice a theme here?)—Beowulf must now fight the real monster, Grendel's evil mother.

HOW TO APPLY THE MONSTER STORY

The easiest story to tell is the monster story because it follows the problem/solution format. The hero is a client who has a big scary problem. Your company is the mentor character who offers a solution. The reluctant hero accepts. The story ends with the hero vanquishing the problem (thanks to accepting the recommendation of the company). And the client lives happily ever after. Here is an example from coauthor Lisa Apolinski.

"My company had used consultants in the past, with very mixed results," marketing director Jessica said. "I was not convinced the cost justified the results."

Jessica had used a consultant for a website project. That project ended up running weeks behind schedule, and she ended up using more of the budget than she anticipated.

"Even with the consultant, the project took on a life of its own," Jessica said.

Jessica had been working in marketing at her organization for five years. She had done well with her initiatives but had hit a wall when it came to using new software for data tracking in order to improve marketing ROI. This expertise was out of her depth. After doing research, she set up a no-cost review call with 3 Dog Write and CEO Lisa Apolinski.

Lisa discussed Jessica's concerns with the project and issues she had with prior projects where outside help needed to be brought in. Jessica's main concerns were making sure data was tracked compared to agreed-upon milestones, and communication on progress was shared using a defined procedure and timeline.

"By having a clear procedure for communication and well-defined milestones, I felt comfortable moving forward with the project," Jessica said. During the course of the project, Jessica was kept informed of progress and how milestones were being reached. During the course of the software implementation, Lisa and her team found several areas to improve current technology use for better integration into the new software.

Jessica worked in tandem with the digital agency, and the implementation process created even stronger systems integration, allowing better data tracking across multiple marketing channels.

"I was so pleased with how well the software implementation went, including being kept in the loop during the entire project," Jessica said of the finished result and overall process.

"Lisa and her team went beyond the original SOW to create value," she said. "The work went well past implementing the software platform and taking that project off of my plate. I learned so much more about the technology integration process. As a team, we discovered other ways to track data and measure ROI. That discovery of additional measures to streamline the process was something I would not have discovered on my own. This experience changed my view of consultants and how I want to work with outside agencies in the future."

UNDERDOG STORIES

No matter what story you tell, the secret ingredient is affinity: can your audience relate to the main character? This is especially true in an underdog story.

This is how affinity is a universal concept that relates to client acceptance, according to a research article by MIT Sloan Management Review[12]:

> We surveyed 3,200 employees in seven industries, including technology, utilities, and finance. Employees who reported being from a stronger culture of companionate love had more job satisfaction, more commitment, and greater personal accountability, and the effect was equally strong for men and women.

EVERYONE LOVES THE UNDERDOG

Back in the days of legal dog fighting, the dog that was winning was called the top dog, and the dog that was losing was called the underdog. People love to root for the underdog. Here are a few examples:

Cinderella (classic fairy tale and two Disney movies). Although the story's title and main character's name changes in different languages, in English-language folklore, Cinderella is the archetypal name. The word "Cinderella" (cinders + beauty) has, by analogy, come to mean one whose attributes were unrecognized or who unexpectedly achieves recognition or success after a period of obscurity and neglect. The still-popular story of Cinderella continues to influence popular culture internationally, lending plot elements, allusions, and tropes to a wide variety of media.

Here is the Disney movie version (the Grimm brothers' version is more, well, grim): Once upon a time in a faraway kingdom, Ella (main character) is living happily with her mother and father until her mother dies. Ella's father remarries, and her new stepmother is a cold, cruel woman (nemesis) who has two mean daughters. When the father dies, Ella's wicked stepmother turns her into a virtual servant in her own house and she is cruelly renamed *Cinder*ella for the fireplace cinders she has to clean up (the name change was reflected in the 2015 live-action film, not the 1950 animated classic).

Meanwhile, across town in the castle, the king determines his son, Prince Charming, should find a suitable bride and provide him with the required number of grandchildren. So, the king invites every eligible maiden in the kingdom to a fancy-dress ball, where his son will be able to choose his bride. Cinderella has no suitable party dress for a ball, but her friends—the mice and the birds—lend a hand in making her one—a dress the evil stepsisters immediately tear apart on the evening of the ball. At this point, enter the fairy godmother (mentor), providing all the tools she needs to get to the ball: the pumpkin carriage, a beautiful gown, and the glass slippers. Cinderella beats the odds to get to the ball and capture the attention of the prince. She then marries Prince Charming and they live happily ever after.

Dodgeball: A True Underdog Story (sports comedy film, 2004). This true underdog story is of the gym owner of Average Joe's—Peter LaFleur (main character)—who has defaulted on his gym mortgage. His small group of members are misfits in society and not welcome in other gyms, including Globo Gym, owned by White Goodman (nemesis). Peter is faced with raising $50,000 in thirty days; otherwise, Goodman, who has purchased the mortgage, will demolish Average Joe's gym to build a parking garage for his facility.

One of the members of Average Joe's suggests they enter a dodgeball tournament in Las Vegas. The first prize is, of course, $50,000. While they are not athletically inclined, they decide this is their one shot. Through the use of a hidden camera, Goodman gets wind of this plan and forms his own dodgeball team to prevent them from winning.

People love to root for the underdog.

During the tournament, Average Joe's team experiences some early setbacks, but makes it to the final round, thanks to the guidance and training by dodgeball legend Patches O'Houlihan (mentor). Sadly, Patches is killed the night before the final round by a falling casino sign. Even on the day of the final match, Average Joe's faces several obstacles. However, they finally have their match with Globo Gym. In a sudden-death face-off, LaFleur beats Woodman by channeling the wisdom of Patches. And since LaFleur sold his gym to Woodman the night before (and bet the proceeds on Average Joe's win—they are in Las Vegas, after all), he comes out $5 million richer, buys a controlling interest in Globo Gym, and unceremoniously fires Woodman. Good guy wins. Big, bad guy loses everything.

David and Goliath. The Bible account of the battle between David and Goliath is told in 1 Samuel chapter 17. The phrase "David and Goliath" has taken on the meaning of an underdog situation, a contest where a smaller, weaker opponent faces a much bigger, stronger adversary. In the Bible account, King Saul and the Israelites are facing the Philistines near the Valley of Elah. Twice a day for forty days, Goliath, the nine-foot-tall giant champion of the Philistines, comes out to the front line of combat and challenges the Israelites to send a champion of their own to decide the outcome in one-on-one combat, but Saul and all the Israelites are afraid. David, bringing food for his older, soldier brothers, hears Goliath had defied the armies of God, learns of a reward for the one that defeats Goliath, and accepts the challenge. Saul reluctantly agrees and offers his armor, which David declines because it is prohibitively heavy, and takes only his staff, sling, and five stones from a brook. David and Goliath confront each other; Goliath, with his armor and javelin, David with his staff and sling.

The Philistine curses David by his gods, but David replies: "This day Jehovah will surrender you into my hand, and I will strike you down, and I will give the dead bodies of the host of the Philistines this day to the birds of the air and to the wild beasts of the earth; that all the earth may know that there is a God in Israel and that all this assembly may know that God saves not with sword and spear; for the battle is God's, and he will give all of you into our hand."

David hurls a stone from his sling with all his might and hits Goliath in the center of his forehead. Goliath falls to the ground and David cuts off his head. The Philistines flee and are pursued by the Israelites. David puts the armor of Goliath in his own tent, takes the head to Jerusalem, and King Saul sends for David to honor him.

HOW TO APPLY THE UNDERDOG STORY

Underdogs do not choose misfortune; misfortune is thrust upon them. Here is a sample story of a client who had challenges similar to what an underdog faces and overcomes.

There was a marketing director named Linda whose situation reminds me of yours. She has been in her position for nearly three years. From the start of her tenure, she dealt with her budget being cut even though her lead generation goals remained the same. The sales team, who would sometimes receive a portion of her department's cut budget, did not have much respect for what marketing could do. She wanted more than to suffer through another year with her budget cuts; she wanted to show the ROI of the marketing channels so her budget would remain intact. Linda worked with our agency and applied two new principles to her marketing strategy. A thorough review of her company's digital channels provided benchmarking and data evidence of the strongest performing channels for lead generation. Her budget was also reallocated based on the data discovery findings to apply every dollar to the best performing channels. With this data, Linda created a digital marketing strategy that provided more qualified leads to the sales team, helping them reach their sales goals quickly. The results were career-altering. She provided data evidence to show lead ROI and subsequent data to ensure budget dollars remained intact. And with more qualified leads, the sales team began to understand the role her department played in their combined success. Linda says her only regret was she didn't call our agency sooner.

[LESSON 7]

COMEDY STORIES

I f you try to solve the problem with a crazy, off-the-wall idea, that is comedy. A true comedy usually ends in romance or marriage. While you probably will not be telling many wacky idea client stories, you should know how they are used. Here are some examples:

Brittany Runs A Marathon (film by Paul Downs Colaizzo). In this hilarious comedy, twenty-eight-year-old Brittany (main character) is a big partier, overweight, and works as a greeter in an off-Broadway theater in New York City. She is given a wake-up call at a doctor's appointment (where she hoped to get another prescription for Adderall): get healthy and lose weight or else. She joins a running group with her seemingly perfect neighbor Catherine, and along with fellow challenged runner Seth, runs her first 5K. To achieve her goal of losing forty-five pounds, Brittany joins Seth and Catherine to train for the ultimate runner's goal: the New York City Marathon (wacky idea). Of course, getting to her goal is not a straight path.

While you probably will not be telling many wacky idea client stories, you should know how they are used.

Tootsie (film by Sydney Pollack). Michael Dorsey (main character) is renowned in the entertainment field for being a good but difficult and temperamental actor. He is informed by his agent George Fields (mentor), that no one will hire him because of his bad reputation. In his personal life, Michael is a bit of a cad who treats women poorly, especially his long-term friend and fellow actor Sandy Lester, a doormat of a woman who already has self-esteem issues.

Both to prove George wrong and to raise money to finance a play written by his roommate Jeff Slater so that he and Sandy can star in it,

Michael goes incognito as a female, Dorothy Michaels, and auditions for a role in the soap opera *Southwest General* (wacky idea) in the role of Emily Kimberley, the tough, no-nonsense administrator of the hospital. As Dorothy, Michael injects into his audition his own sensibilities, which lands him the short-term role. As Michael progresses in the role, only George and Jeff know Dorothy's identity. As Dorothy, Michael continues to play the role as he himself would, often ad-libbing. He detests his director Ron Carlisle (nemesis) for the way he treats "her" and women in general (much the way Michael treated women himself), including Ron's girlfriend, lead of *Southwest General* actress Julie Nichols. Dorothy treats Julie with care and respect and begins to fall in love with her. However, two men fall for Dorothy, namely *Southwest General*'s longtime lothario lead actor John Van Horn, and Julie's on-screen father, Les. Michael must find a way to let Julie know his feelings without ruining their friendship. Worse problems arise for Michael when Dorothy's no-exit clause contract on *Southwest General* is extended, meaning Michael may have to pretend to be Dorothy for much longer than he was originally intending.

Some Like It Hot (film by Billy Wilder). In the winter of 1929, Chicago friends and roommates Jerry and Joe (main characters) are band musicians—a string bassist, and tenor saxophonist, respectively. They are also deeply in debt. Smooth-talking womanizer Joe is a glass-half-full type who figures they can earn quick money to pay off their debts by gambling with the little money they earn. More conservative Jerry is a glass-half-empty type of guy. They are in the wrong place at the wrong time when they witness a gangland slaying by bootlegger Spats Colombo (nemesis) and his men. Jerry and Joe manage to make it away from the scene within an inch of their lives.

Needing to lay low and get out of town away from Spats, they sense an opportunity when they learn of a local jazz band needing a bassist and a saxophonist for a three-week gig at a luxurious tropical seaside resort in Miami, all expenses paid. The problem? This is an all-girl band—but nothing that "Geraldine" and "Josephine" can't overcome by dressing in disguise as women (wacky and oddly repeatable idea), the former of whom instead chooses Daphne as "her" stage name. Sweet Sue, the band leader, has two basic rules for band members while on tour: no liquor and no men. Beyond needing to evade Spats and his henchmen and maintain the front of being women (especially in the most private of situations with the other female band members), Jerry and Joe have two additional problems.

First, the more brazen Joe falls for one of the other band members, ukulele player and vocalist Sugar Kane Kowalczyk (although Jerry, too, is attracted to her). Joe does whatever he can to find time to get out of drag to woo Sugar while in Miami, using all the knowledge Josephine gleans directly from Sugar about what floats her boat in potential-husband material. And second, Jerry, as Daphne, catches the eye of wealthy love-struck Osgood Fielding III, who doggedly pursues "her" and won't take no for an answer. The last line of the movie is one of the greatest in the history of cinema. As Shakespeare would say, "all's well that ends well," with this comedy of errors.

HOW TO APPLY THE COMEDY STORY

The key to a comedy story is talking about solving a problem with a wacky idea. Consulting can be a serious task, so you might want to lighten the mood. Here is a story from coauthor Lisa Apolinski.

When Trevor attended my webinar, he had a lot of digital content already, with some reasonable engagement. With the global pandemic and subsequent economic disruption, he wanted to make sure he was creating enough content. When I told Trevor that he would need to rewrite nearly all of his digital content on his website, he thought that was a wacky idea (and may have used more colorful language). Trevor made the choice of working with our agency to redo his entire digital engagement strategy. The new strategy took several weeks but had an immediate impact on overall digital engagement and lead generation. Trevor was happy but, at the same time, wished he had called us sooner. "Thank you for your guidance, but I have to admit, this has been a comedy of errors," said Trevor. "Knowing the right way to develop digital content is as important as having content. This would have saved a lot of extra effort." Nobody wants to completely redo all of their digital content, but sometimes a wacky idea like a new digital strategy is the only solution for an all's-well-that-ends-well outcome.

TRAGEDY STORIES

I f a person tries to solve a problem by going against the laws of society or nature or the universe, that is a tragedy. The decision to take a shortcut is a tragic decision, and shortcuts usually do not work out in the end.

As noted earlier, the tragedy doesn't readily lend itself to client stories. That's because it's a harsh cautionary tale with no room for hope, lessons learned, or redemption until it's far too late for any of the characters. They tend to end up dead in pools of blood due to their own poor decisions.

Most companies do not want to envision that type of a future—bankruptcy, lawsuits, or a combination of the two. They also do not want to have a consultant or vendor suggest they may be choosing a shortcut that leads to a bad decision since a bad decision equals lost revenue.

We do not recommend tragedy stories for those reasons. A client success story is a much better bet. But, to fully illustrate the tragedy story, here are some examples.

Othello (play by William Shakespeare). A 1500s Venetian general, Othello (main character), allows his marriage to be destroyed when a vengeful lieutenant convinces him that his new wife has been unfaithful. Iago (nemesis/ mentor), a Venetian army officer and ensign to the Moorish general, Othello, bitterly resents the appointment of Cassio as Othello's chief lieutenant. Iago, and minor character Roderigo, maliciously bait Brabantio, an old senator. Before the council chamber, Brabantio accused Othello of abducting his daughter to elope with her. Othello denies this, and Desdemona affirms loyalty to her new husband.

Iago (here is the problem—Othello lets his nemesis also be his mentor) assures Roderigo, who is also secretly in love with Desdemona that she will not love Othello for long. Iago brings Desdemona to Cyprus to celebrate Othello's victory against the Turks and incites Cassio and Montano into a drunken brawl. Montano is seriously hurt, and Iago beckons Othello, blaming Cassio, who is dismissed from duties. Iago then advises Cassio to seek Desdemona's assistance in regaining Othello's favor. Iago arranges for Othello to find his wife in earnest conversation with Cassio, and subtly arouses the Moor's jealousy by creating a slanderous piece of evidence, placing Desdemona's handkerchief (an intimate item) in Cassio's possession.

Othello's fatal flaw is believing Iago's lie that his lieutenant, Cassio, has been cuckolding him—a lie that leads to a tragic end. Othello ultimately kills Desdemona in a jealous rage and commits suicide himself. Cassio also gets a decent stab in the leg for his pains, and when Iago's wife realizes he's behind the whole thing, she exposes him, and he kills her. Other bodies pile up along the way as well. Iago himself survives the carnage and vows never to explain why he decided to set in motion all these horrible acts in the first place.

Most companies do not want to envision that type of a future—bankruptcy, lawsuits, or a combination of the two.

King Lear (play by William Shakespeare). King Lear (main character), old and tired, divides his kingdom among his three daughters, giving great importance to their elaborate declarations of love for him. When Cordelia, the youngest and most honest, refuses to idly flatter the old man in return for a favor, he banishes her and turns to his remaining daughters for support. But older daughters Goneril and Regan (nemesis characters) have no actual love for him and instead plot to take all his power from him. In a parallel plotline, Lear's loyal courtier Gloucester favors his illegitimate son, Edmund, after being told lies about his faithful son, Edgar. Madness and tragedy befall both ill-fated, but prideful, fathers. They even hang King Lear's court jester (mentor), a fool who spoke the truth to the king.

Parasite (film by Bong Joon-Ho). This 2019 South Korean black comedy (another way to say tragedy) was the first foreign-language film to win the Academy Award for Best Picture. The Kim family struggles to make financial ends meet in their semi-basement apartment. The son of the Kim family, Ki-Woo (main character), starts the chain of events for this family's rise and fall. Using a forged diploma from Yonsei University, Ki-Woo is hired as an English tutor for the daughter of the wealthy Park family and starts to look for opportunities to bring in other members of his grifter family. His sister Ki-Jung poses as Jessica, a sought-after art therapist who takes up working with Park's young son Da-song. Each family member recommends the next to fully infiltrate the Park household to take as much money as possible.

The one worker standing in the way of the Kim family's takeover is the longtime housekeeper Moon-Gwang (nemesis), who returns one evening when the Park family has left for a trip. Moon-Gwang pushes her way into the home to access the underground bunker in the basement. Her husband has been in this bunker for years hiding from loan sharks after his bakery failed and left him with massive debt. What follows is a series of bad decisions by nearly all members of both families. Unsurprisingly (it is a tragedy), the body count is high (Ki-Woo's sister Ki-Jung, Moon-Gwang and her husband, and Mr. Park). In the end, Ki-Woo suffers severe brain trauma and undergoes brain surgery, he and his mother are convicted of fraud, and both end up back in the same semi-basement apartment they were so desperate to escape. The patriarch of the Kim family, Ki-Taek, having killed his employer, Mr. Park, is now in hiding in the underground bunker. He sends a daily message to his son in Morse code using the outside lights and sneaks into the kitchen for food, constantly in fear of getting caught by the new owners of the house.

Ki-Woo, further behind the curve than ever before, vows to make enough money to purchase the home, free his father, and reunite his parents once more.

HOW TO APPLY THE TRAGEDY STORY

A tragedy story is a cautionary tale. The key to this story for case acceptance is talking about how a great tragedy was avoided.

Avoiding the dentist can have tragic consequences. The hero of this story is Michael's mom. Michael was four years old when his mom noticed a small bulge in his cheek. Putting off going to see health care providers is not unusual. But Michael's mom decided to take him to the pediatrician, who then referred him to his dentist. Upon evaluation and x-ray, Michael was scheduled with an oral surgeon to remove what appeared to be a cyst under his tooth. That cyst turned out to be more serious than anyone anticipated. Within twenty-four hours, Michael was admitted to St. Jude Children's Research Hospital in Memphis, Tennessee, where he began a year-long battle with leukemia. This story has a happy ending: due to early detection and treatment, Michael is doing well and has just graduated from college. He is now interviewing with St. Jude in the marketing department to help save the lives of other children.

MYSTERY STORIES

Whodunnit? Either the audience is in the dark along with the hero, or the audience knows the answer and wonders how and when the main character will figure it all out.

In conversations with business executives, the audience usually does not know the answer. The mentor guides the hero into the world of digital data to discover the truth. Even in the current world of Big Data, many companies still miss opportunities to utilize collected data to solve business issues. Mystery stories are a clever way to bring in evidence-based decision-making (data) into a conversation with a client.

Here are examples:

The Hound of the Baskervilles (novel by Sir Arthur Conan Doyle, plus many film versions). Sherlock Holmes (main character) is a consulting detective in Victorian London. When Sir Charles Baskerville dies unexpectedly, his nephew and heir, Sir Henry, returns from South Africa. Dr. Mortimer, the local doctor, is concerned about Sir Henry's safety, as he is convinced that Sir Charles was frightened to death. He consults detective Sherlock Holmes and recounts the tale of one Sir Hugo Baskerville who, several generations previously, had been killed by a huge hound and which now is believed by some to be a curse on the family. Holmes agrees to take on the case, and it almost immediately becomes apparent that Sir Henry's life is in danger. Holmes doesn't believe in the legend of the Baskervilles or the alleged curse placed upon them and sets out to find a more practical solution. (Interesting story fact: Sherlock Holmes holds the Guinness World Record for the most portrayed literary human character in film and TV.) Spoiler alert: Holmes *always* solves the case.

Mystery stories are a clever way to bring in evidence-based decision-making (data) into a conversation with a client.

Murder on the Orient Express (novel by Agatha Christie, 1974 film directed by Sidney Lumet, 2017 film directed by Kenneth Branagh). Unexpectedly returning to England from Istanbul in 1935, famed Belgian detective Hercule Poirot (main character) finds himself traveling on the luxury train, the Orient Express. One of the passengers, Mr. Ratchett, informs Poirot that he has been receiving anonymous threats and asks Poirot to act as his bodyguard. Poirot declines, but when Ratchett is found stabbed to death the next morning, it is apparent that the threats he had received were real. Poirot soon deduces that Ratchett was, in fact, the infamous Cassetti, believed to have been the man behind the kidnapping and murder of three-year-old Daisy Armstrong five years previously. As he begins to question the dozen or so passengers on the train, he realizes several of them have a connection to the Armstrong family, and he begins to form a solution to a complex crime. And the murderer is . . .

HOW TO APPLY THE MYSTERY STORY

A mystery story is about a riddle, a puzzle, or unlocking a code. Drop words like that and include secret, clue, and detective work into the story to appeal to the listener.

It was a mystery to Paige, the CEO of an equipment manufacturing company, why a typically robust digital channel was suddenly underperforming, even though they had added new email addresses to the platform. She told us she had focused on creating email campaigns to increase website traffic. With the new emails, she had reasoned her campaigns would drive more traffic. She was puzzled when the opposite occurred.

Paige mentioned she had purchased the email list to assist with this effort and was concerned the email list was the cause. After some digital detective work, we told her the email list needed further segmentation, and new copy would be tested against these new segmented audiences. Paige scheduled the services, and within several weeks, her email campaign project was complete. She was thrilled with the results and said her only regret was not getting the assistance sooner. "I thought my decision to purchase the list was the issue," said Paige. "I was so happy to learn that list segmentation and targeted communication were the secrets to optimizing this investment."

[LESSON 10]
QUEST STORIES

Quest stories are about a journey to find a great prize, or to use Joseph Campbell's word, a boon. Perhaps the prize is to rescue someone, recover something, save the world, or obtain some treasure. Maybe the real treasure is the knowledge you learn along the way. Many memoirs are quest stories.

Here are some classic story examples:

Indiana Jones and the Raiders of the Lost Ark (a film by George Lucas and Stephen Spielberg). The year is 1936. Archeology professor Indiana Jones (main character) narrowly escapes death—by poison dart, a fall, and finally, a giant boulder that chases him out a cave in a South American temple after obtaining a gold idol. An old enemy, René Belloq (nemesis), steals the idol and then orders a group of natives to chase "Indy" down and kill him. Indy, however, escapes back to the United States, where Army intelligence officers are waiting for him at his university. They tell him about a flurry of Nazi archaeological activity near Cairo, which Indy determines may be related to the possible resting place of the Ark of the Covenant—the chest that carried the original Ten Commandments. The Ark is believed to carry an incredibly powerful source of energy that must not fall into Nazi hands.

Indiana is immediately sent overseas, stopping in Nepal to pick up a relic his old professor had that may hold the key to the Ark's location (and also his former girlfriend Marion, his old professor's daughter), then meeting up in Cairo with his friend Sallah. But danger lurks everywhere in the form of Nazi thugs and poisonous snakes in the Ark's resting place. After Belloq, hired by the Nazis, beats Indy to the treasure again, this time the Ark, Indy and Marion are determined to get it back, and they overpower the pilot of a German plane.

But Indy finds himself confronted with a giant German thug, and after a frightening hand-to-hand fight, Indy and Marion blow up the plane. Now the Nazis must drive the Ark to Cairo, but Indy regains control of the Ark after running the convoy off the road, one vehicle at a time. Once again, the Nazis recapture the Ark—and Marion—and head for a Nazi-controlled island. There, Belloq will open the Ark to demonstrate the horrific power it can unleash upon the world.

Maybe the real treasure is the knowledge you learn along the way.

Galaxy Quest (film directed by Dean Parisot). With their 1980s show canceled, the cast of the television series *Galaxy Quest* have fallen to making appearances at conventions. The show's former lead star, Jason Nesmith (main character), constantly hungover and barely making it through the appearances, is hated by his former castmates but loved by fans. When Jason is transported to an exact replica of the

NSEA Protector by a group calling themselves Thermians, he believes he needs to simply act as the captain and gives half-hearted orders to the crew.

The Thermians call on Jason the following day, this time with the rest of the cast present. When all of them are transported to the Protector, Jason finds out that his "orders" caused the near extinction of the Thermians by the evil warlord Sarris (nemesis). After several mistakes, Jason and his crew pull together with a superfan of the show to take on Sarris and his men. They also learn to appreciate the impact the show has in the universe, their role within the television series, and their bond as a family. Jason, in particular, rediscovers his passion for acting and how important fans are as the lifeblood of a series. Most importantly, he finds his purpose after being rudderless.

HOW TO APPLY THE QUEST STORY

A quest story is about a journey in search of a prize of great value. There is a call to the quest for the client, and you are the guide on their journey. This is an example from coauthor Lisa Apolinski.

Paul called our offices last year. He was on a quest to develop a strong strategy to meet his department's revenue goals, even in the midst of a merger of two strong competitors.

"I am not sure if it is possible to obtain revenue growth in this environment," confessed Paul. "Should I revise our revenue goal? What can I do to stay on track and drive my team toward success?"

We knew the journey was not going to be easy. Paul would have to review his digital content and how he presented the value of his products.

"Good news, Paul: Your company can still accelerate revenue growth by creating new content in the form of storytelling. This content would then be shared through a revised channel mix," I told him.

Paul was skeptical at first. He was also not looking forward to having to develop new marketing content. Based on our discussion, he decided to move ahead with the new digital engagement strategy.

The quest was not achieved overnight. However, after nine months, Paul had implemented a new digital engagement strategy and saw the impact of digital storytelling on revenue growth.

He told us: "Thank you. Our revenue goal is in sight, and we have the momentum to get there. What's more, my team is motivated to stay the course, and we are

*working together to create our digital
story. Together, my team will be able to
use these strategies, even in the face of
strong competition."*

REBIRTH STORIES

What was dead has come back to life. Like a phoenix rising from the ashes, a person or institution is born again. In the world of business, many "mess-to-success" stories are actually rebirth stories. An individual realizes that s/he should break out into the world with a new company after encountering setbacks in a current career situation.

Here are some examples:

A Christmas Carol (story by Charles Dickens and many film versions). On Christmas Eve, crotchety miser Ebenezer Scrooge (main character) is visited by the ghost of his dead partner Jacob Marley. Scrooge is told that what one does in life will determine what happens to them in the afterlife. Marley tells Scrooge that he will be visited by three ghosts (mentor characters) and to take heed of what happens. The first spirit, the Ghost of Christmas Past, shows Scrooge was once a happy young man, carefree and in love, but money became his greatest desire. The Ghost of Christmas Present shows him how others, including his nephew, Fred, and his clerk, Bob Cratchit, are spending a poor but loving holiday together, as well as Tiny Tim's crutch by a fireplace. The Ghost of Christmas Yet to Come shows Scrooge the fate that awaits him. Scrooge learns from his visits and becomes a good man who knows how to celebrate Christmas—as well as how to live better all year long.

Like a phoenix rising from the ashes,
a person or institution is born again.

Good Will Hunting (story by Matt Damon and Ben Affleck, directed by Gus Van Sant). Will Hunting (main character) is a foul-mouthed, short-tempered janitor at MIT who is also a self-taught genius. Professor Lambeau posts a math problem on a hallway blackboard to test his graduate students, and janitor Will is the one able to solve the problem. The professor goes to speak to Will, who is now in jail for assault. If Will agrees to study mathematics under the professor and go to therapy sessions, he can avoid further jail time.

Will outsmarts all of the therapists he sees until he meets Dr. Sean Maguire, an old classmate of Lambeau's and someone from the same South Boston neighborhood as Will. Maguire (mentor) challenges Will and his defense mechanisms starting in the first session, where Will insults Maguire's dead wife and has to face the consequences of his words (something he has not had to do because of his superior intelligence and quick comments). He meets a girl, Skylar, but has a hard time letting down his guard with her because of his troubled past and ends up breaking her heart.

Slowly, Will's defenses are broken down by Maguire after they find out they were both victims of child abuse. Will takes a leap of faith and goes after Skylar in California, now open to a new future after having passed up a prestigious job offer arranged by Lambeau. He lets Maguire know that he has gone "to see about a girl," a line Maguire used when he gave up his ticket to the 1975 World Series Game Six after he saw his wife for the first time and fell instantly in love with her.

Cast Away (a movie directed and coproduced by Robert Zemeckis). Tom Hanks stars as Chuck Noland (main character), an analyst at FedEx who is too busy focusing on resolving productivity problems to be present in the lives of his coworkers or even his longtime girlfriend, Kelly. His work takes priority and he has to fly to Malaysia on Christmas before he is able to propose to Kelly. (He says the famous line, "I will be right back.")

On the way to Malaysia, the plane encounters a terrible storm, making the plane crash into the Pacific Ocean. Chuck barely makes it to a deserted island, and when he cuts his hand trying to make fire, he creates a bloodied handprint on a Wilson volleyball (which he names Wilson). During the four years he is on the island, he and Wilson (the mentor character) have nothing but time on their hands. When a portable toilet section washes up on the island, Chuck devises a plan to get past the surf and be rescued. During the journey off of the island, Wilson is lost to the sea, leaving Chuck despondent. However, a passing ship sees and rescues Chuck.

Back in the United States, Chuck learns how much has transpired, including being declared dead. His coworker's wife passed away from cancer, and Kelly married someone else and had a child—time has moved on without him. A coworker (whom he had taken for granted before) comes to his hotel room after Chuck's final encounter with Kelly. Chuck relays how he had to let Kelly go for good, and that nothing was ever under his control, including time.

Chuck then goes to deliver an unopened FedEx package decorated with angel wings that had washed ashore and leaves it at the house with a note saying the package saved his life. At a deserted crossroads, he encounters a woman in a pickup truck who tells him where each road leads. As she drives off, Chuck sees angel wings on her truck, similar to what was on the FedEx package he had just delivered.

HOW TO APPLY THE REBIRTH STORY

A rebirth story is about a journey that ends in redemption for the main character. Here, coauthor Lisa Apolinski travels through a difficult situation and finds the power within to transform the situation (and herself) with the help of a mentor.

The year was 2013; the place was Milan, Italy. After having worked another fourteen-hour day, Lisa sat in her hotel room, exhausted and frustrated. She called her sister, and that call altered her career path.

"I should feel lucky to have a job where I am able to travel and where I am successful," Lisa shared. *"But days like today, where I spend hours trying to explain basic marketing to senior executives who won't listen, are awful. How can I keep giving my best in an environment like this?"*

Her sister asked her about her side work, and Lisa's demeanor changed. "Oh, it is great! I am helping a former vendor with content for his new company website. He loves my ideas!"

"How do you feel when you do this side work?" her sister asked.

"I love it. I get to help set marketing strategies in the right direction, and my ideas are always appreciated. I feel like a superhero."

"Then maybe you should be focusing on your side work full-time," her sister responded.

That conversation planted a seed: What could a career beyond the corporate horizon look like? Nearly a decade later, Lisa is one of the top digital growth experts in the world. She has taught (and her wisdom is sought by) thousands of senior executives across four continents. Her understanding of digital growth, especially during unpredictable times and economic uncertainty, has provided her agency with the foundation for expansion. And yes, her clients listen to her expertise.

[LESSON 12]
ESCAPE STORIES

Many films have escape right in the title: *Escape from New York*, *The Great Escape*, and *Escape from Witch Mountain* come to mind. An escape story starts in a normal place, goes to a crazy place, and then the characters must cheat death and make it back to a normal place—home. As Glinda the Good Witch teaches Dorothy Gale in Oz, "There's no place like home" (could have used that advice when the house landed on the first witch, but oh, well).

Here are some examples:

Edge of Tomorrow (film directed by Doug Liman). Major William Cage (main character) is a PR officer who has zero combat experience. He is told he will be covering the final battle against an alien invasion (nemesis) on the front lines, but when he refuses, he is forced into a battle squad by a general. He dies during that battle but also kills an alien mimic in the process—a rare one that gives him the ability to reset the day, knowing what has already transpired. He joins forces with battle-worn warrior Rita Vrataski, a.k.a. The Angel of Verdun (mentor character). He becomes a true soldier and fighter, training with Vrataski and dying every day in the mission to find a way of defeating the extraterrestrial beings before they find Cage and take back the ability to control time.

An escape story starts in a normal place, goes to a crazy place, and then the characters must cheat death and make it back to a normal place—home.

Gone with the Wind (novel by Margaret Mitchell and film produced by David O. Selznick). This epic tale of the Old South from the start of the Civil War through the period of reconstruction focuses on the beautiful Scarlett O'Hara (main character). Before the start of the war, life at the O'Hara plantation, Tara, could only be described as genteel (except, of course, if you were a slave). As for the young Scarlett, she is, without doubt, the most beautiful girl in the area. She is looking forward to a barbecue at the nearby Wilkes plantation, as she will get to see the man she loves, Ashley Wilkes. She is more than a little dismayed when she hears he is to marry Melanie Hamilton, and in a fit of anger, she decides to marry Melanie's brother. The Civil War (nemesis) is soon declared, and as always seems to be the case, the men march off to battle, thinking it will only last a few weeks. Now living in Atlanta, Scarlett sees the ravages that war brings. She also becomes reacquainted with Rhett Butler (later the mentor character), whom she had first met at the Wilkes barbecue. Now a widow, she still pines for the married Ashley and dreams of his return. With the war lost, however, she returns to Tara and faces the hardship of keeping her family together and Tara from being sold at auction to collect the taxes. She has become hardened and bitter and will do anything, including marrying her sister's beau, to ensure "with God as my witness," she will never again be poor and hungry. After becoming a widow for the second time, she finally marries the dashing Rhett, but they soon find themselves working at cross-purposes, their relationship seemingly doomed from the outset. Rhett leaves with a classic *Oh, snap* exit line. Scarlett realizes that even if she doesn't get Rhett back, she can always return to her land—escape back to Tara. As Scarlett says: "Tara! Home. I'll go home, and I'll think of some way to get him back! After all, tomorrow is another day!"

HOW TO APPLY THE ESCAPE STORY

The escape story is about being in a normal place, going to a crazy place, and getting back to normal. You are telling how the hero escaped a bad situation. This is similar to the rebirth story. Here is an example from coauthor Lisa Apolinski.

One of our other clients, Pete, found himself in a situation similar to yours. He had seen a few years of revenue decline in his company and some of his resources cut as a result, and that can be hard to escape. After years of losing market share, a unique opportunity came along: There was a disruption with his competitors and a potential opening in the industry. But success would not be easy.

"I saw that my company could regain a foothold in the industry, but was not

*sure how to do it with a reduced budget,"
said Pete.*

*Preparing a strong digital growth
strategy with limited funds was a bit
daunting. Pete needed to get some
additional sales to justify a request to
increase marketing funds. He contacted
3 Dog Write to see how a strategy could
be developed for "quick wins" on a
limited budget to get the ball rolling.*

*The good news: 3 Dog Write's Digital
Discovery Process provided Pete with
strong data analytics that showed several
areas with good potential for revenue
generation and only needed small
tweaks (and did not take a huge amount
of financial investment to achieve).*

*Pete was motivated by this information
and, armed with evidence-based decision-
making, created a plan to leverage these
opportunities. The plan worked amazingly*

well. What was the end result? In a matter of weeks, Pete increased website traffic and lead inquiries. In addition, this new plan shortened the lead conversion cycle (an average of 18 percent), getting leads across the finish line to a sale.

That is how Pete escaped the trapping of a reduced budget and leveraged new industry conditions to accelerate his company's revenue growth. If Pete's story resonates with you, we would love to put together a plan to help your company take market share.

THREADING THE DIGITAL NEEDLE

Persuading with a digital content story is not limited to longer communication, such as an email, an article, or a webinar. Every piece of digital content that you create for your company has the power to persuade if the content leverages digital storytelling.

Even content as short as a tweet can clearly cast a role in the story and driving the storyline forward. For example:

Here I come to save the day!

Mighty Mouse takes on the hero role, which leaves the content consumer in the role of damsel in distress.

Do or do not. There is no try.

The powerful words of Yoda, our mentor character, provide guidance and a choice for the hero in this story.

RANDOM ACTS OF CONTENT?

Many organizations today create content because it either sounds good or feels good. As long as you are creating content, does it matter why? Well, of course, it does! Every piece of content created is an opportunity to speak to your potential customer. There should never be random acts of content: all content has a purpose.

Just as your story matters, so does your digital content. Fortunately, every company can create a digital content strategy. This seven-step template was developed from the work and wisdom of digital sales transformer Bernie Borges (and is shared with his permission). He is cofounder and CMO of Vengreso and the host of the award-winning *Modern Marketing Engine* podcast.

Every piece of digital content that you create for your company has the power to persuade if the content leverages digital storytelling.

STEP ONE:
CREATE YOUR MISSION STATEMENT

A mission statement is critical in the alignment of your communication with your goal. Every time a piece of communication or content is created (email, video, article, etc.), it should be checked to make sure it follows the mission statement. This is an internal statement kept within the team.

At [insert business], [insert your audience; *who* will read your content?] will find [insert adjective; *what* type of content will you create?] content for [insert the result; *why* will your audience consume your content, and *what will the result be?*].

STEP TWO:
DISCOVER YOUR TARGET AUDIENCE'S NEEDS

List the top three to five things that your target audience is looking to do. Your communication should address one of these needs. Not sure what the audience's needs are? You can always ask.

STEP THREE:
MAP YOUR TARGET AUDIENCE'S JOURNEY

Your audience will go through several stages before they trust your communication and decide to take action (whether that be to purchase, volunteer, donate, etc.).

For each of the stages below, what will the content provide that is in alignment with the needs listed above? Where do each of these needs fit in the journey (and it can be more than one stage), and how can the content address these needs?

1. Awareness: when they discover you and what you have to offer

2. Consideration: when they are reviewing your communication and content to decide if what you provide aligns with what they need

3. Decision: when they make the decision to take action (this can be the most critical—communication does not stop when they have taken action; support after the action can create an advocate for your company)

STEP FOUR:
IDENTIFY THE ROLE OF CONTENT FOR THE EXTENDED TEAM

Your extended team (sales, support staff, volunteers) can also use content to provide information and messaging. What role do you envision for your content to support your extended team and provide them with information and talking points?

STEP FIVE:
CHOOSE YOUR CONTENT FORMATS

Content can take on several formats. What are the top six to eight formats you plan on using? Data information at this stage can help you decide on the formats.

Content formats can include:

- Video

- Success stories

- Blogs/articles

- Email

- Third-party information (sharing information from other credible sources)

STEP SIX:
PLAN FREQUENCY OF CONTENT

How often do you plan on publishing and sharing content? Frequency should be benchmarked by how well the audience responds to content and others in your industry. For each format, list how often content will be published.

Remember, this is a preliminary document, and frequency will change as more data is gathered.

STEP SEVEN:
MEASURE CONTENT SUCCESS

For each of the content formats, how will you measure success? What data points will indicate a piece of content or a format is performing well? Many benchmarks for content formats are available online. In addition, tracking data will also provide an indication of improvement in engagement.

Don't forget to review how well the content addressed the audience's identified needs. Have additional needs or questions come out of the content that should be added?

Overall, how do these pieces of content feed into your ultimate goal, whether that be revenue, increased attendance, or better community engagement?

By putting a digital content strategy in place, every piece of content that you create and share fits into both your digital story and your drive to the company goal.

THE IMPORTANCE OF CEO DIGITAL STORYTELLING

The last week of February 2020 marked the beginning of a new economic climate. The Dow Jones Industrial Average[13] dropped over the next several weeks to lows not seen since November of 2016, with the largest single-day drop (1,191 points) recorded on February 27, 2020. The first case of COVID-19 was detected in the United States in February[14] as well, and by mid-March, every state had at least one case; a national emergency[15] was issued by the White House on March 13, 2020.

In the ensuing weeks, as the pandemic was being felt around the world, many countries ordered citizens to shelter in place, and nonessential businesses were required to close. In April 2020, the United States unemployment rate jumped to 14.7 percent[16].

With most of the world staying home and engaging with others mostly through digital means, the importance of the digital story was thrust into the spotlight. Many large brands tapped their CEO to send out a personal email or video message on what processes and procedures were being put into place so that when the world "opened" again, customers would feel comfortable engaging in pre-pandemic activities—things as benign as going to a store, working out, flying, eating at a restaurant, or staying at a hotel.

Many CEOs realized their job in this new normal would be to speak directly to customers and employees. A group of eleven forward-thinking CEOs came together in a Zoom CEO Roundtable Focus Group in early May 2020 and discussed one burning question: How are you communicating your company story in the new normal?

THE CORE THEMES

The first core theme that came up in the CEO Roundtable: Companies need to show value to the customer more than ever.

> *You have to bring something to the table that solves just their problem. And now this is the time compression point: it is inside of the next sixty days, which is as far out in their future as they trust.*
> *—Tom Searcy, Hunt Big Sales*

> *If you think about what's happening, it's about using digital with human touch to reach out and proactively reassure clients that their portfolios will be okay, for example. That, even though the bank branch is closed, they're still open for business, and this is how you can access your funds. As a software company, we always used to say we're not curing cancer.*

> *But in the last sixty days, our customers have told us that we've saved lives because we've allowed bankers and insurance agents, these essential businesses, to be able to close and actually perform their work from home.*
>
> *—Clara Shih, Hearsay Systems*

> *Many CEOs realized their job in this new-normal would be to speak directly to customers and employees.*

Another core theme: Moving outside your CEO comfort zone is critical now, and that includes shifting your focus to new ways of being.

> *The 15 percent of business leaders are going to help the 100 percent navigate this, possibly for the next few years. There are going to be other challenges. It's time for us all to step up to a whole new level. And in order for us to do things we've never done, we have to become people we've never been.*
>
> *—Susan Sly, Radius AI*

Everything is centered on how we can educate, share, and show up. One of the things that we're doing to show up is to be still and listen to what's happening with our audience and our prospects. Instead of running in and trying to talk about our story, we want to focus on our audience and make our story and our needs second—to be quiet and be present.
—Lisa Apolinski, 3 Dog Write

I've personally jumped in as a salesperson. I think the team seeing me out actually visiting stores in the area just to make sure that it's safe and to help has been really critical. My employees are seeing the executive team do things that they don't typically do.
—Kara Golden, Hint Water

The last core focus was the CEO as Chief Energy Officer: to give and find inspiration from different points of view.

From my perspective as a CEO, the number-one job is to inspire and energize. And

CEOs now have to look at their business through two lenses: a microscope and a telescope. My focus is to revive, renew, and refresh the purpose, the goal, and the mission. And to revive, in the minds and the hearts of everyone in the company, the "why" they are here.

—Feyzi Fatehi, Corent Technology

We came together as a company to say what we're doing can help both women and the community. Let's make sure we continue to focus on what we control and how we can impact women everywhere. One of our values is giving back. We can do something to help our community. So, we joined an innovation coalition, donating elastics, which we use on our bras, that are now being used for masks.

—Heidi Zak, ThirdLove

WHAT IS COMING ON THE DIGITAL HORIZON?

T he economic uncertainty is something we have faced in the past and will most certainly face again in the future. The question then becomes not *if* the digital landscape will change, but *when*. The next discovery is on the digital horizon—something just beyond our reach and drawing closer every day.

There has been much debate, speculation, and assertions in this "COVID era," a term dubbed by Bernie Borges, digital marketing thought leader and host of the *Modern Marketing Engine* podcast. He has commented that content must be "more relevant, more empathetic, and more helpful" than the pre-COVID days.

In the recent past, organizations would push out content, regardless of quality or applicability, to have potential customers respond. Companies, in turn, would say they were authentic and relevant to their content consumers. When a new economic, political, environmental, or health crisis hit, those companies would react by shifting their content message to whatever they believed to be the appropriate response. Their desire to supply content, any content, drove the strategy.

The next discovery is on the digital horizon— something just beyond our reach and drawing closer every day.

If you have received or seen any of those content pieces in this COVID era, the underlying message was always the same: "We say we are here for you, even if you have not heard from us in months, if ever. What we really want is to ask of you, yet again, for your time, money, resources, talent, etc. And our gift in return is our gratitude . . . maybe."

LET GO OF THE BANANA

Wild monkeys are captured in an interesting way: A crate full of bananas is left out in the open. The slots in the crate are wide enough for the monkey to reach in, but not wide enough to extract one of the bananas. The monkey will reach in to grab the banana but will refuse to let go. So, the monkey is "tethered" to the crate by its own refusal to let go of the prize, thus ensuring its capture.

When it comes to digital content, many organizations are blind to their refusal to simply let go of the banana and thus avoid a bad situation (I don't know what happens to those monkeys, but I cannot imagine it is anything good).

This also means the ability to persuade with a digital content story lies within you, waiting to be tapped. However, you must realize your hand is in the crate in order to let go of the prize. This is the easiest step in the process, yet the hardest step to achieve.

In order to persuade with a digital content story, companies must turn their strategy on its head. What role are you assigning yourself, and what role is the audience playing in your digital engagement? How is your state of being affecting the digital content story you tell?

Attempting to anticipate the shifts in consumer behavior, economic upheavals, and the digital landscape will be frustrating and, most likely futile. Focus instead on the digital story you wish to share, and how that story provides value to your audience.

How do you know what your audience needs or considers to be of value? The easiest way to find out is to simply ask. By providing a path for your audience to share what is relevant to them at this moment, they have a means of sharing what their current pain point is. Creating and sharing content that helps your audience address that current pain point not only creates lasting value but allows the audience to be heard. This may not be an immediate sale, but providing long-term relevancy and a clear understanding of your customer will lead to repeat revenue, no matter what storm is brewing on the horizon.

Remember, you have a story, and your story matters. Instead of selling, provide a story for your audience on how they can beat that monster/achieve that prize/be reborn into the hero hidden within.

People are hardwired for stories, especially digital content stories. And there is no better time to share your digital story than right now.

[APPENDIX]
ACKNOWLEDGMENTS

From Lisa Apolinski

Special thanks first to Henry DeVries and the Indie Books International Inc. team. Henry constantly raises the bar for me in my professional work, and for that I am begrudgingly grateful. Also, thanks to Sonja Hunter, my best friend. She has been a sounding board for my ideas and thoughts, and always provides helpful and direct feedback (i.e., she doesn't let me go off the stupid-ideas cliff). Lastly, thanks to all my past, present, and future clients. Seeing you go out into the world to make digital content better keeps me in the fight.

From Henry DeVries

Special thanks to the Indie Books International Inc. team of Vikki DeVries, Mark LeBlanc, Ann LeBlanc, Devin DeVries, Denise Montgomery,

Joni McPherson, Kylie Strem, Suzanne Hagen, Jordan DeVries, and more. I get to be out front as the quarterback, but without their efforts, I would be flat on my back. Yes, a football metaphor from a baseball nut. I owe a debt of gratitude to my story-loving buddy Michael Hauge for many grand discussions about Hollywood, which he calls "the emotion picture capital of the world." Appreciation goes to my San Diego State University graduate advisor, the late Dr. Glen Broom, who was my mentor for four decades, and a much-missed golf partner. I am grateful that I got to call the greatest mind in the field my friend. He taught me to do well by doing good.

ABOUT THE AUTHORS

Lisa Apolinski is the CEO of 3 Dog Write Inc., a full-service digital consulting agency she founded in 2012. She works with businesses who want to accelerate revenue and take market share using digital means. As a speaker, she teaches business leaders how to affect sales growth with their digital content strategy. In the last eight years, she has helped her clients create nearly $1 billion in revenue growth. Her first book, *Weathering the Digital Storm*, has been used by businesses around the world to fortify their digital growth strategies in unpredictable times. Because of her thought leadership on digital engagement, she has been dubbed "America's Digital Content Futurist."

As a result of working with 3 Dog Write, companies get the three Rs: *realignment* of resources, *reengagement* of lead funnel, and a customized plan for *realizing* revenue gains.

On a personal note, Lisa sang opera for many years, including touring with a Chicago-based opera company. She continues to sing as a music minister in her church.

You can invite Lisa to speak on how to persuade with a digital content story by emailing her at lisa@3dogwrite.com. You may not get her to stop.

Henry DeVries is the CEO (chief encouragement officer) of Indie Books International, a company he cofounded in 2014. He works with independent consultants who want to attract more high-paying clients by marketing with a book and speeches. As a speaker, he trains business leaders how to sell more services by persuading with a story. In the last ten years, he has helped ghostwrite, edit, and coauthor more than three hundred business advice books, including his McGraw-Hill best seller, *How to*

Close a Deal Like Warren Buffett—now in five languages, including Chinese. He has authored or coauthored twelve marketing books and writes a weekly column for Forbes.com.

As a result of working with him, professionals, consultants, and business leaders report they enjoy more impact and influence.

On a personal note, Henry is a baseball nut. A former Associated Press sportswriter, he has visited forty-three major league ball parks and has two to go before he "touches 'em all." His hobby is writing comedy screenplays that he plans will one day be made into films. You can invite him to speak about persuading with a story or go to a baseball game by emailing henry@indiebooksintl.com or calling 619-540-3031.

ENDNOTES

1   "How Many Blog Posts Are Published per Day - 2020 Statistics." HostingTribunal, February 28, 2020. https://hostingtribunal.com/blog/blog-posts-per-day/.

2   "35+ WordPress Statistics: It Rules Supreme in 2020." HostingTribunal, February 28, 2020. https://hostingtribunal.com/blog/wordpress-statistics/.

3   Zheng, David. "The 15 Second Rule: 3 Reasons Why Users Leave a Website." The Daily Egg, May 25, 2020. https://www.crazyegg.com/blog/why-users-leave-a-website/.

4   Kemp, Simon. "Digital Trends 2020: Every Single Stat You Need to Know about the Internet." Podium | The Next Web, February 6, 2020. https://thenextweb.com/podium/2020/01/30/digital-trends-2020-every-single-stat-you-need-to-know-about-the-internet/.

5   Escalas, Jennifer Edson. "Self-Referencing and Persuasion: Narrative Transportation versus Analytical Elaboration." *Journal of Consumer Research*, March 2007, Volume 33, Issue 4.

6   Green, Melanie, Garst, Jennifer, Brock, Timothy, and Chung Sungeun. "Fact Versus Fiction Labeling: Persuasion Parity Despite Heightened Scrutiny of Fact." *Journal of Media Psychology*. 2006. Volume 8, issue 3.

7   De Jager, Adele, Andrea Fogerty, Anne Tewson, Caroline Lennette, and Katherine M. Boydell. "Digital Storytelling in Research: A Systematic Review. *The Qualitative Report*. Volume 22, Number 10 (2017).

8   Smeda, Najat, Eva Dakich, and Nalin Sharda. "The Effectiveness of Digital Storytelling In The Classrooms: A Comprehensive Study," *Smart Learning Environments*, Volume 1 Article 6 (2014).

9   Rosilie, Grace Ann, David M. Boje, and Donna M. Carlon. "Storytelling Diamond: an Antenarrative Integration Of The Six Facets of Storytelling in Organization Research Design," *Organizational Research Methods*, Volume 16, Issue 4 (2013).

10   Gallagher, Kathleen Marie. "In Search Of A Theoretical Basis For Storytelling In Education Research: Story As Method." *International Journal Of Research & Method In Education*. Volume 34 (2011).

11   Woodside, Arch G. "Brand-Consumer
     Storytelling Theory And Research: Introduction
     To A Psychology & Marketing Special Issue."
     Psychology & Marketing. (May 13, 2010).

12   Barsade, Sigal. "Employee Emotions Aren't Noise
     — They're Data." *MIT Sloan Management Review*,
     November 6, 2019. https://sloanreview.mit.
     edu/article/employee-emotions-arent-noise-
     theyre-data/.

13   "DJI Interactive Stock Chart." ^DJI Interactive
     Stock Chart | Dow Jones Industrial Average
     Stock - Yahoo Finance. Accessed July 7, 2020.
     https://yhoo.it/3iiQV2N.

14   "United States COVID-19 Cases and Deaths by
     State." CDC COVID Data Tracker. Centers for
     Disease Control and Prevention. Accessed July 4,
     2020. https://www.cdc.gov/coronavirus/2019-
     ncov/cases-updates/cases-in-us.html.

15   "Proclamation on Declaring a National
     Emergency Concerning the Novel Coronavirus
     Disease (COVID-19) Outbreak." The White
     House. The United States Government. Accessed
     July 7, 2020. https://www.whitehouse.gov/
     presidential-actions/proclamation-declaring-
     national-emergency-concerning-novel-
     coronavirus-disease-covid-19-outbreak/?utm_
     source=link.

16   "United States Unemployment Rate 1948-2020"
      webpage. Data: 2021-2022: Calendar (Forecast
      tab). Trading Economics. Accessed July 7, 2020.
      https://tradingeconomics.com/unitedstates/
      unemployment-rate.

Made in the USA
Las Vegas, NV
30 March 2021

20414948R10094